The Oligarch Loses

Claudia Daventry

Templar Poetry

Published in 2015 by Templar Poetry

Fenelon House
Kingsbridge Terrace
58 Dale Road, Matlock, Derbyshire
DE4 3NB

www.templarpoetry.co.uk

ISBN 978-1-906285-79-1

For permission to reprint or broadcast these poems write to
Templar Poetry

A CIP catalogue record of this book is available from the British Library

Typeset by Pliny

Cover Design and Artwork by Templar

Printed in England

Acknowledgements

The Oligarch Loses His Patience won the inaugural Roehampton Ruskin Prize and appeared in POEM 2015. *Longbarrow* appeared in Hallelujah for the 50ft Woman, Bloodaxe 2015, *Homing* in Magma 2014, *We Are Part Star* in the Island Review 2013., *L'Autrichienne* second place in the Philip Larkin/ East Riding prize 2014, *Perspective* appeared in the Bridport Prize anthology 2007, *Leaving Amsterdam* in the Arvon prize anthology 2006, *Brood* in the Troubadour Café Poets 2013, *Alakazam* won the 2012 Bridport Prize. Several of the poems were longlisted in the National Poetry Competition.

to Tilda, Inés and Eve, with love – always

Contents

The Oligarch Loses His Patience

This is for the time she put sugared lime peels
in the bonbonnière. Then served sherbert
in the spindled glasses with the silver filigree
handles and sprinkled over crystal violets
with hammered tongs twisted from sheets
of tin stolen from his mines. The time she pinched
a fingerful of coca from his snuffbox, sniffed
it through a rolled *billet-doux* slipped
from her garter; the times she used this *petite*
cuillère (warmed round an artisan's thumb)
that dangled on the velvet ribbon tied around
her pale throat – its scorched underside,
a few grains of powder clinging to gold
beaten so thin you could hear it scream.

Longbarrow

Beauty's on the inside, so they say, but they don't know —
who can judge my clutch of soft and pulsing organs
that pump — flux-stop-reflux — gouts of astonished blood
in cyan and magenta round the scaffold
of my bones, my meat and my dark caverns? Who's to say
these creamy glands, two butter beans in sanguine sauce,
these devilled kidneys, dark as plums, my lover's liver
glistening like a deepsea conch, this duodenum,
crinkled, damp and pocketed as purple wrack
or the twin seaslugs of my lungs that plunder air
are lovelier or more temperate than another girl's?

Skin-deep's more legible. So now let me enhance
the parts that, underneath this skin, are less than taut
and translate nature's failings with synthetic sympathy
building a shrine in silicone to my elastic youth.
When they stumble on my longbarrow and dig me up,
they'll find my parchment in a randomness of sticks,
my bowl of skull, fissured with fine occiput craquelure,
two black stare-holes. My gaptooth grin. Tangled
in the nuggets of my vertebrae Mum's locket
and on the birdcage of my ribs will sit two jellyfish,
pristine, intact, pert as the day they were slipped in.

The Duel

At the moment that I grip my wand
before I raise it to your mask of spit and bile
an incantantion brightens in my mind
like daybreak over hills, or distant sail
on a flat horizon, not so much in word
but fluid understanding: that to be still
is not to exorcise the low thrum of rage
but to unroot the parasite that grows inside
the hollow self – that fills us with illusion,
petrified, through years of 'know' and 'want',
swelling to the solid oak-bole of our will
that darkens every window with its girth –
to free the space is to let in light.

Homing

Here's to the two who, coupled, could grace
the marble hollows of a double tomb, yet
they rise and part at the *selva oscura*.

One stands on the spit looking out to sea,
staggers in spray, drenched by the surge
and swell, a heave and massive chuck

of the wave over the shoulders and head,
the keen blade of onshore wind that grazes
throats and wrists. The other has no fat, is spare,

burns down wood to the last embers,
no char, no ash blowing in an empty grate;
wades through cold beneath a parting curlew,

must rake the sand to upturn a shell.
Both say to the spit-roast or to the lares, *no*;
no to wall-to-wall, *no* to knowing the warmth

in the bed beside them is daily bread, no
as intimacy's sweetness turns to chalk. Yes
to the chance meeting, sweet nick of a scalpel,

to a shriek on a higher frequency. To sift
a nugget of truth from the white noise of talk,
of giving it all up for a single shaft of flint, cool in the palm; for

the upturned bottle and a slur of *eau de vie*,
for a stab of pain at the musk of new sweat
and who come back, again and again,

to the unwritten contract, unringed like wild birds
migrating across continents, who return
to the crumbling ledge, who cover miles but mate for life,

who, giving in to the force that drags them home
– windswept, roadweary, sore with the roil of salt –
test the raw edge of what might even be love.

We are part star

We are bone and water stretched out, prone
before the burning logs, made soft by wine,
the slow-twitch movement held by skin

— not two lovers, bellies to the rug, but
a necromancer's toss of jumbled runes.
A shake and pitch, whose message burns

through broad oak planks and beams, through panes
and out into the night of sodden leaves and loam,
skimming, with September's ghost, the darkened lawns,

glancing off sandstone pillars, past the clean
sweep of the drive, across the bay to Eilean Arainn,
shedding embers on a sleeping ptarmigan

then, humming, bounces off Goat Fell, airborne,
soaring through cold ether, lit by moon
and fogged with smoke; nothing, now, between

the lovers who never loved and the black sun.
We're grounded. I felt your heartbeat in the stone
even as our feet slipped in wet clay; the pain

releasing as we climbed the glen,
stole brown water from the tumbled burn:
drank deep of rusty iron and peat and rain

and grasped at trees whose roots will scream
when they're dragged, too soon,
from the soil of sleeping Earls. It's sin,

Yggdrasil says, to mess with so much *rún*
– your life is not your own. The night turns:
we are the flint that sparks the dawn.

L'Autrichienne

She felt alone. She missed the Court, her dog,
she couldn't understand the way they spoke,
the lack of kindness in their perfect food,
the way they stuffed their geese with grain until
the liver burst, the bland and nutty paste
they served with brioche toast and moscatel,
the paper cone they used to hide her face
when powdering her hair, the ruches, whalebone
and the laces of the corset, pulled
to snap against the eyelets with her gasp,
the hairline-fractured rib, and how her breasts,
pressed flat as champagne saucers, sprang
to freedom like a pair of *sans culottes*
— flushed to the tips with red, *enragés*; young.

perspective

There are days when I am so
clumsy I step into the street and I
knock over trucks with my hip

without noticing. Days when you are
not there. Days when I feel
the weight of love with none of its

levity, when I am watching your
solo flight as you shake me,
in a shower of mercury droplets, free

and feather out your span from tip to tip
spiralling up into the ether
where the spot that is me, miles below

stands in its clogs
and wonders, dully,
what happened to the binoculars.

The Snug

Where were you born, he said, I said, in Fife,
which was a lie: it was in London. And
what was your life? he said. I said, oh, this,
and that, and more of that. He said, that's not
enough, so, what's enough, said I. It means
I want to know who bore you through the foam,
who rocked you in your shell, who warmed your nacre
bed before you went to sleep, who took
 your hand and held it when the moon sucked out
its blood and left it still and white with fear
of ghosts that come to sip the wit from your ears.
I want to know, he said, leaned in and scried
the pupils of my eyes for injury,
for telltale evidence, for marks and scars

and locked me in his pewter stare, his rain,
where, like a shilling dropped in a well –
the dark splash, its ripples that spread out;
I saw the knuckles of the big fists
that made him taste the sour-penny red
of his own blood, felt the heat of shame
rise, stood on a box before twenty boys –
his deepscored errors hung around his neck
by a pale master with chalkdust in his gown
who lived in sin with algebra and mockery –
the pants his mother ironed too flat, the wrong
shoes, the girl who laughed him off the dancefloor,
the guffaws of the chum who quietly ripped
him off, the wife who took the smack to her jaw.

Leaving Amsterdam

To break away is relative.

I packed the rugs, the bed – and then
I threw the bedroom in.

I pushed in the wormy boards and beams
that have seen 400 years: the horses first,
with steaming flanks and rolling eyes
brought in unshackled from their shafts.
I packed the hay
the dust of hay
I packed the groom, the stable boy
the bridles and the bits.

I packed the puritan who beat his wife
behind closed doors.
I packed the doors
and, with them, the scream
she let out as he kicked her down
the steep black stairs.

I packed his kick.

I packed six Jews from beneath the floors;
pale as onion shoots, and thin
as gruel. Packed their dim
lamp, its paraffin
and seven Nazis thumping up the steep black stairs
to drag them out.

I packed the guns.

The Kerkstraat came up easily
once I'd loosed the cobbles from their bed
and rolled up the street, like liquorice.

The houses came, stretching soft as caramel
as I gently tugged them from their roots
which, after all,
are only clutching at water.

The Oligarch's First Wife Looks On

She watches from behind drapes as he hauls
his upholstered bulk up on the battened flanks
of one of his best tanks: the parade shine
on his fine leather boots, which, as a rule
means Sergei will keep his job, for the time
being – though what time is nowadays, the banks
being the way they are and *the Chicago school*
to all intents running the IMF, they slur, after wine
and over armagnac
                                    and the kind of cigars
rolled on the inner thighs of imaginary señoritas
much younger than she is, now, whose burnished
and eternal legs fold into bucket seats of cars
with more souplesse than her shapewear-moulded frame
can manage. In short, she's finished.

Child

The day the drag–lift shut
the snow was gathering in fog
that clotted on the looming peaks,
stranding me with a nigh-no-choice,

—   to push you under the old byre wall and wait
 the blizzard out, or make like Wenceslaus
and strike out down blind fells of drift and crag,
your life a bird in my fist.

                    I still feel the clutch
of fear's nails in my viscera,
as I led you off the piste, into a glare
of white. The hairline, darting across
our shelf of ice like a bad promise.
That tiny, toytown ricochet.

Catch i

and I think when the catch came in she fell in love
with the sea or the salt or the mud or the roots
of the trees or the white of his skin in the cold of
the water the rock where she slipped and the blood

that was red they should know should know better her wean
back home greeting the eyesore the woodsmoke and close
now and closer the thigh and a hip shy of touching
that burns as they drag the catch high on the beach

and filleting mackerel a catch in her breath
leaning over the knifeblock — her twin at the door
and his eye's like a gimlet she's paring the blade
and the scream of the steel is too bright to the gut

how it felt when they danced with his fist in the small
of her back on her skin and his knuckles were kneading
her backbone like banging a bodhrán she felt
like a hare like a hare with her pelt stretched too tight

way too thin at the surface the beat of the hand–heel
that thuds out the rhythm her own man too close
to the dance for much comfort or safety the milk
for her wean rising into her breast

and it soaks through her shift with the fright of that heat
in the curve of her back and the discs of her spine
shucked together like oyster-shells singing a language
that jangles her cortex that tells her it's wrong, but

the music is fast and the music is loud
and the whisky's still rolls in her head like a bowl
and it rolls as she spins by his arm by his arm
as he throws her away pulls her in like the catch.

Brood

Niamh has ghosts. It started when he left for the city.
The night she went outside to feed the hens, and found
them – stone-cold, paralysed, stiff in their own shit
without a trace of blood, no damage to the ground
or snippage to the chicken-wire, no sawdust in their food –
a frisson stung her back like a drop of cold sweat.
Niamh has big hands. The night the chickens died
she fetched a shovel from the shed and dug a pit.
She scooped the feathered bodies to her breast,
each one in turn; buried her thumbs in the neck–ruff,
lifted wings, but found no cuts, no sores, no marks at all:
no singed pentangles, kabala, no runes in their trough,
but she knew. As she laid each one in earth, she crossed
herself, kissed her fingers, and committed him to hell.

Boundaries

are tanks really more important than pears?

Milan Kundera

She said, *the tanks are coming* – with their treads
that flatten mud and rocks and celandine
and liles by the waterside, that crush
the garden walls between the neighbours,
bitter now for thirty years, a kind of love
that's grown from loathing for the colour of
her sweetbriar or the trellis on the fence
he put up for his wife which blocked
her early morning sun, and how she cuts
her hedges; close as nailquicks, trim
but dense with twigs, too dark, he said *the tanks,*
how can this be, and in a rush of blood
remembered all the times he hid behind
the upstairs nets to watch her kneel and clip
and coax her tender shoots and how her skirt
was tight across her haunches, how it stirred
his loins while downstairs, by the warm range,
dough was proving for tomorrow's bread,
the floor was scrubbed of footmarks but his children,
barefoot in the garden, playing hide
and seek amongst the pear-trees shrieked
each time those hedges scratched their skin.

Backstory

Yael lives beneath my floorboards
and puts me right when I swither, judge
too softly, take less than my share –
it's I who put her there, and I must answer for
her righteous pain, her keening wail for gruel,
the darkness in her spidered corners, where
she kvetches at the clang of the convent bell
and nags to live outside with me in light,
away from pisspots, matches, tapers; free
from predators who want to snap her life
or trap her in the fields or factories, a rope
around her neck or iron ring on her foot
with rusting links that clink and rub her raw
each time she tugs to pull herself away.

Shlomo's music's in my wainscot – hear
the double-stops, harmonics and
the sliding thirds in his lament. Mice
block ears and deathwatch ticks teem
for the cracks between the planks
and how they run, and how they try
to disappear – but nothing with a pulse
can creep into a space that's small
enough to shelter from that shrill
top E, the flatted fifths he plays
to frighten us – that's why he does it,
right? – reminding us mortality
comes to us all. His devil's tritones
needle blood from my nailbeds.

Blot

We don't want to overpathologise normals, but
he saw a *chameleon* in card eight,
which you might expect if he were French
– we know the English see cats and dogs –
and we're not certain whether it is significant
that he refers to a *troll* rather than an *ogre*
in card four. Card seven he saw *human*
which is a standard response in Japan
and North America but not here, where
research has shown high preference for *spider*.
As it happens, our clinician is also bilingual
which caused some confusion in card three
as, for her, a bow tie is also a *butterfly*,
the cause of the aberration being semantic,
merely; an internalisation by the examiner,
not the indication of above-average creativity
one finds in the artistic population (as opposed
to the non-artistic normal population): *nota bene*
the *unique response* has a positive correlation
with amygdalar enlargement. Concerns with sex:
his response *bra* was categorized under *clothing*
by the female clinician though on a second reading
our psychologist, Max, felt it to be repression,
perhaps, given that he found *buttocks*
in the *wolf's head*, also latent homosexuality.
On card six he claimed *Christmas Elves*
which, since it is not Christmas and he is not
Scandinavian, is, we think, worthy of comment.
Card one was unequivocal. He just gave us *bats*.

Armistice

In times of war remember how,
behind the disused armaments hangar
there is buddleia

where butterflies tangle and scatter dew.
That, as mortars release their soft crump
and thud from miles away

houses fold in on their hearths; paper games
of marriage-beds are crushed by falling masonry.
Remember the two planes that spun out

and landed in fields separated by razor-wire.
As the dust floats down, remember
to seek out the black box of who I meant to be.

Alakazam

It wears no cloak, but its lining is purple silk. It spills
and churns with the caps of onshore waves
spoiling the white froth of Normandy lace. It is the dirty slick
– black, thick – that clogs feathers, air; bug-eyed creatures gag on it.

It is the furthest point on any horizon, through a telescope.
The skew of the horoscope. The blackfanged fish, a mile down,
grimacing with crush-barrier spines through the thick lens of a bathyscope,
pulled along by its pallid light. The boom of the deep. It is

rougher than a panther's tongue and smoother than birch-bark.
It rings like a silver spoon on crystal, gold as a gypsy's tooth
in a travelling fair. It has mud in its ruts and ice on its tips,
its bones rattle in a dry wind and its coffers are packed with dull stones

each one heavy as a curse. It is bread: not the twice-baked crust
but the slow steam of heat, torn from the heart. It is
the fringe and hoof of a carthorse that sparks off flint. Is flint.
It is the chalk and rock of powdered cathedrals, of ground bells,

of light bled through red and green-stained panes, of myrrh, thorns and tears;
it is rinsed with grief. It is the isthmus, the strait, the bridge,
the monolith, the ruined feet of the colossus. It is a drift of fine sand
across the ruins, the blue night of the desert and its cold sliver of moon,

it is the last dram, the full cup, the explosion of an hourglass on a slate floor.
It is long-distance, the slowburn, the thin air of the altiplano,
a barely perceptible pulse. It is a windfarm. On Arizona asphalt,
it is the tumbleweed, the skull and the last few drops in the sump

and it won't be pulled out of a hat by its ears.
The conjuror lays his wand in velvet. Peels off his moustachios.
The crowd is looking the other way; there is no more *Alakazam*.
Love jumps out and darts under the table.

The Catch ii

— was that it was the burn we heard:
just nature, ripping off the muffled roar
of air-conditioning outside
the bedroom window, sending phantom
restaurant smells of last night's greasy
washing up and slippy floors,
of waste-disposals, pork-rinds, bones
and fish-heads bursting from the split
in weak grey garbage sacks.
I'm a clinging wrecked fortress round
the contours of the bed (because some limb
of yours was flung akimbo, taking
too much space the way you always take),

I hate those couples on romantic trysts
who knot their fingers on a linen cloth
and share a misprint on the menu, or
make tiny goblets out of foil, because
they had each other, just as some might think
that I have you. How could I say
to waiters stepping up to pour,
it wasn't how it looked, it wasn't
such a catch, the thing we had,
that even though the cognac swayed
in crystal globes that faintly boomed
to chime the *sláinte*, underneath
the tabletop your hand caressed a gun

named brother, womb-sharer and twin.
I dreamed you woke and found me gone,
my shallow dent still warm, my hollow
skull-shape scooped out of the pillow,

all the cast-off things you nailed me with –
magpie-glints and ringpulls, bridge between
the world and what you let me know of it
– I couldn't stand that thing you'd do
when it hit home I'd slipped my chain
and broken for the hills. How, then,
you'd push that muzzle up inside your chancer's mouth,
and in the tumult of the burn you'd squeeze
the catch and burst your head apart.

Scheveningen

'Pass the salt', I say, and you hand me the knife,
with the house reflected *à l'envers* in its blade –
careless, as Oscar Wilde might have said,

knowing, as I know you do, that before the knife
you should have given a penny, fifty cents,
a *dubbeltje*, an obol – any currency keeps at bay

the bad spirits which come between the blade
and the recipient and severs good blood forever.
Notice now in these few lines how I return the knife

to you, not once but in every *strophe*, making damn sure
you can hear the double stops sliding up the strings
in your darkness, and then you see the shadow of the knife,

now quivering a little, on the shower curtain of your life
– this same knife, so you know what it is to be made a stranger
in your own home, your words turned to butter in your mouth.

The Fetch

This was an evening made of milk, late
air furred with a film of harvest-dust
and I stepped out to walk the coast-path
into town. My town – a bled smudge,

the haven of home behind me,
between the two a long stretch of tar
gone mellow in the sun, treacle-black,
loading the air with the dark whiff of pitch.

Nothing strange about this, you may say,
and I would say, at any usual dusk,
to brush top-heavy blooms of cow-parsley,
scattering motes of pollen, in a haze

of floating seed – rose-bay willow-herb,
late red campion, warning snakes away;
dog-flowers, buttercups dipped with bees,
I would say the same: nothing strange,

so in the lengthening shade I was unready
for the jolt that stopped me dead
when I met, coming the other way, myself.
My heart lurched like a trapped bird

battering against its cage of rib, breath
gone to rags. There is nothing on earth
– nothing – that can prepare a soul
for the nameless horror (like vertigo

spiked with a dash of grave-rot)
of discovering you are not
who or what you thought – the composite
of your loves, your losses, your dreams,

your version of a world that made sense
when there was a you-shaped hole
in it to accommodate the real, only you,
through muscle-twitch, nerve-pulse, *tic*.

I stopped: both of me stopped, and
considered the other – if other we were.
'But – where are you going?' we said
with the double timbre of the soon-dead

though as the words left my mouths I knew
there is no answer: this is a fleeting errand
– sooner or later we see whichever way
is wrong; that we are no-one.